RAINFOREST

EDWARD R. RICCIUTI

MARSHALL CAVENDISH

NEW YORK

Benchmark Books
Marshall Cavendish Corporation
99 White Plains Road
Tarrytown, New York 10591-9001

©Marshall Cavendish Corporation, 1996

Series created by Blackbirch Graphics, Inc.

Printed in Hong Kong.

Library of Congress Cataloging-in-Publication Data

Ricciuti, Edward R.
    Rainforest / by Edward R. Ricciuti.
       p.   cm. — (Biomes of the world)
    Includes bibliographical references (p.   ) and index.
    ISBN 0-7614-0081-8 (lib. bdg.) — ISBN 0-7614-0078-8 (set)
    1. Rain forest ecology—Juvenile literature. 2. Rain forests—Juvenile literature. [1. Rain forests. 2. Rain forest ecology. 3. Ecology.] I. Title. II. Series.
QH541.5.R27R53   1995
574.5'2642'0913—dc20   95-4021
                                                      CIP
                                                      AC

Contents

Introduction

People traveling in an airplane often marvel at the patchwork patterns they see as they look down on the land. Fields, forests, grasslands, and deserts, each with its own identifiable color and texture, form a crazy quilt of varying designs. Ecologists—scientists who study the relationship between living things and their environment—have also observed the repeating patterns of life that appear across the surface of the earth. They have named these geographical areas biomes. A biome is defined by certain environmental conditions and by the plants and animals that have adapted to these conditions.

The map identifies the earth's biomes and shows their placement across the continents. Most of the biomes are on land. They include the tropical rainforest, temperate forest, grassland, tundra, taiga, chaparral, and desert. Each has a unique climate, including yearly patterns of temperature, rainfall, and sunlight, as well as certain kinds of soil. In addition to the land biomes, the oceans of the world make up a single biome, which is defined by its salt-water environment.

Looking at biomes helps us understand the interconnections between our planet and the living things that inhabit it. For example, the tilt of the earth on its axis and wind patterns both help to determine the climate of any particular biome.

The climate, in turn, has a great impact on the types of plants that can flourish, or even survive, in an area. That plant life influences the composition and stability of the soil. And the soil, in turn, influences which plants will thrive. These interconnections continue in every aspect of nature. While some animals eat plants, others use plants for shelter or concealment. And the types of plants that grow in a biome directly influence the species of animals that live there. Some of the animals help pollinate plants. Many of them enrich the soil with their waste.

Within each biome, the interplay of climatic conditions, plants, and animals defines a broad pattern of life. All of these interactions make the plants and animals of a biome interdependent and create a delicate natural balance. Recognizing these different relationships and how they shape the natural world enables us to appreciate the complexity of life on Earth and the beauty of the biomes of which we are a part.

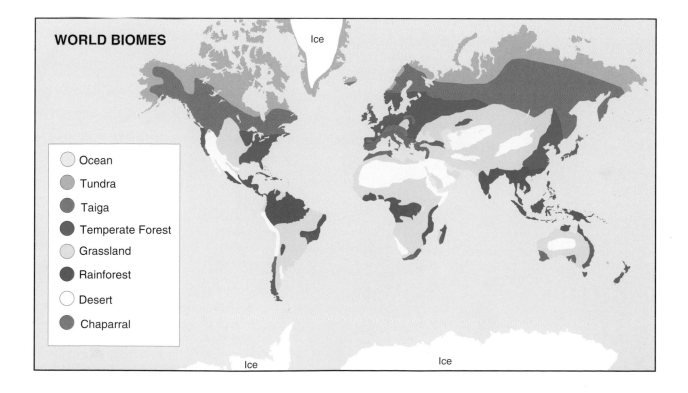

WORLD BIOMES

Ice

- Ocean
- Tundra
- Taiga
- Temperate Forest
- Grassland
- Rainforest
- Desert
- Chaparral

Ice

Ice

1
A Greenhouse World

Nairobi, Kenya, is less than 300 miles (483 kilometers) from Africa's east coast, on the Indian Ocean. Douala, Cameroon, can be found on Africa's west coast, on the shore of the South Atlantic Ocean. If you were to take a jetliner from Nairobi to Douala, you would fly virtually straight across the middle of Africa, almost right above the equator. For the first hour of your trip, you would look down on Kenya's grasslands, dotted here and there with trees. As you traveled farther west, the grasslands would gradually disappear and the stands of trees would grow thicker. For the next four hours or so, you would pass over a blanket of green, broken only by an occasional river or settlement. No matter where you looked, you would

Opposite: When flying over Costa Rica, you can see the thick canopy of the rainforest below.

see only the tops of trees, stretching to the horizon. This is the tropical rainforest of central Africa, which totals more than 460 million acres (186 million hectares). Despite its vastness, it is the third smallest of the world's three major rainforest areas. The second largest, at more than 600 million acres (243 million hectares), is the rainforest of southeast Asia and includes such islands as the Philippines and New Guinea. Largest of all is the rainforest of tropical America (Central America and South America), which totals almost 1,370 million acres (555 million hectares) in size. Smaller regions of rainforest can be found in other parts of the world, such as northeastern Australia and some of the Caribbean islands.

The Great Jungles

Tropical rainforests make up a biome found only in the regions between the Tropic of Cancer, north of the equator, and the Tropic of Capricorn, south of the equator. This biome once covered more than 7 million square miles (18 million square kilometers). Today, although many areas of rainforest have been destroyed by human activities, the biome spans almost 4 million square miles (10 million square kilometers). The rainforest biome has a climate similar to that of a green-house. All rainforests have warm temperatures and high humidity that vary little over the course of a year. Temperatures in the rainforests change by only a few degrees from season to season, because in the tropics the sun's light is more evenly distributed throughout the year than it is in the temperate and the polar zones. Humidity is often close to 90 percent for days at a time. Rain soaks these forests about five days out of every week, although it does not rain all day long. The rainforest has the most stable climate of any biome on Earth.

Rainforests have average temperatures of at least 75° F (24° C). Although always warm, rainforests seldom get as hot as New York City or Phoenix, Arizona, can get during a summer heat wave. The amount of rain a rainforest needs to thrive is no less than 80 inches (203 centimeters) a year. Some, however, get 288 inches (732 centimeters) of rain or more.

Some other tropical forests clearly resemble rainforests. Parts of southern Asia have seasons of very heavy rain and wind that last for several months. These are called monsoons. However, for three or four months of the year, these areas have a dry season. Even so, the vegetation remains lush because of the huge amounts of rain that fall during the monsoon. Such forests are called monsoon forests, or seasonal tropical forests. Another kind of forest, the montane forest, grows on the middle slopes of some tropical mountains. This forest contains many of the same trees as the rainforest does, and is also wet throughout the year. But winds and cooler temperatures make the montane forest less productive in plant life—and, therefore, animal life—than the true rainforest, which is usually found at lower elevations.

All of these forests are commonly known as the jungle. The ancient Indian word from which "jungle" is derived refers to a biome similar to that of the rainforest today. The Indian word, jangala, means "impenetrable tangle of trees." Eventually, jangala became "djanghael," used to denote dry areas of thick, thorny scrub and small trees. After the British arrived in India, they began to use the word for many wooded areas, including the rainforest.

Life in Layers

The vegetation of the rainforest is divided from top to bottom into five different zones, or layers. The zone farthest from ground level is the emergent layer, a name that comes from the trees that emerge far above the rest of the forest. The heights of both the trees and each rainforest layer vary from region to region. In general, however, most emergent trees are 130 to 250 feet (40 to 76 meters) high, with their lowest branches often 50 feet (15 meters) above the ground. Some of their crowns spread to an acre in size.

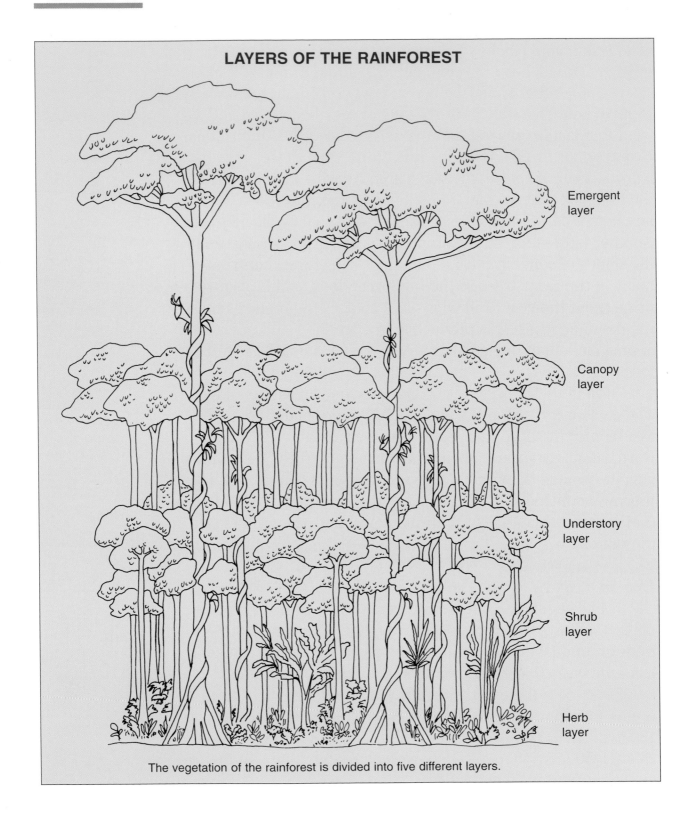

LAYERS OF THE RAINFOREST

Emergent layer

Canopy layer

Understory layer

Shrub layer

Herb layer

The vegetation of the rainforest is divided into five different layers.

Below the emergent layer, at a height of between 65 and 130 feet (20 and 40 meters), is the canopy layer. Here, the crowns of trees are very near to one another, even touching. Huge vines called lianas, which are often hundreds of feet long and interlaced throughout the canopy, connect the branches of different trees. It is the canopy that gives the rainforest the appearance of a continuous blanket of green when it is seen from above.

The canopy has a great influence on the forest beneath it. It shields the area below from the wind and the impact of rain. Its shade prevents the lower levels from becoming too warm during the day, and, like a blanket, it keeps in heat at night. Because of the canopy, about 98 percent of the sunlight shining on the rainforest is lost before it reaches the ground. For this reason, vegetation on the forest floor is sparse, except where breaks in the canopy allow light to enter, and along openings made by rivers. The shores of rainforest streams are often walled by a tangle of vegetation.

Directly under the canopy is the middle, or understory, layer. It is dense and composed of the trunks of emergent and canopy trees, smaller trees with narrow crowns, vines, and young trees fighting to grow higher. In this layer are the tops of buttress roots, triangular plates of wood that extend from the trunks of

Rainforest soil is rich in nutrients only a few inches deep. This causes most rainforest trees to have shallow underground roots. These triangular buttress roots help to anchor the enormous trees of the rainforest.

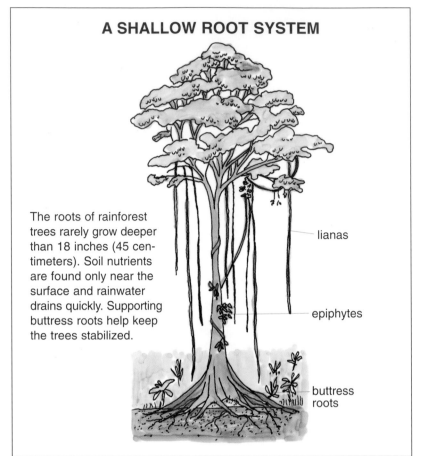

A SHALLOW ROOT SYSTEM

The roots of rainforest trees rarely grow deeper than 18 inches (45 centimeters). Soil nutrients are found only near the surface and rainwater drains quickly. Supporting buttress roots help keep the trees stabilized.

lianas

epiphytes

buttress roots

tall trees and make them resistant to the winds and storms that batter the emergent and canopy layers. About 20 to 30 feet (6 to 9 meters) above the ground, the shrub layer begins. Thinly spaced shrubs, which are cut off from the light above, make up this zone. The forest floor, or ground level, is called the herb layer. Herbs are low, nonwoody plants, and because they do not receive any sunlight, most of the herb plants on the forest floor are small. These soft plants, however, would have a difficult time surviving in the hot sun, driving rain, and winds if the canopy did not shield them.

In a way, the floor of the rainforest is like the floor of the deep sea—the abyss. Little grows here due to lack of sunlight. Food comes from above in the form of fallen leaves and branches, animal droppings, and the remains of dead animals. These organic materials are decomposed by fungi, bacteria, and other organisms that convert them into nutrients. Even so, the topsoil of the rainforest floor is only a few inches thick, and poor in nutrients. How, then, does it feed the mass of vegetation in the forest? First, decomposition occurs very quickly in the rainforest because of the heat and moisture. Second, since the soil is thin, the roots of the trees are spread out close to the surface. They quickly absorb the nutrients into the trees themselves. In fact, most of the nutrients in a rainforest are found in its vegetation, not in its soil.

Plants and Animals Aplenty

The constant heat and humidity of the rainforest biome promote an explosion of plant life. This abundant vegetation supports, in turn, a vast number of different animals. Some scientists estimate that half the living species, or kinds, of plants and animals on Earth inhabit the rainforests.

Studies done in Borneo have shown that just a couple of acres of rainforest can contain 700 different species of trees, compared with fewer than 20 species per acre for even the rich North American forests. The rainforests of the Amazon Basin in South America, for example, are home to more than 50,000 plant species. Just one tree in the Amazon Basin can have 80 other species growing on it.

A rainforest is like a cafeteria. It offers one kind of plant food for one species of animal, another kind for a different species. The plant eaters then become food for the meat eaters. Because there are so many different types of food in the rainforests, a tremendous number of different animals inhabit them.

A 10,000-square-mile (25,900-square-kilometer) area of rainforest, for example, might have four times the number of bird species living in it year-round than a comparable area in North America would have. The animals most abundant in the rainforests, however, are the insects, especially ants. Rainforest ants live both below the ground and in the trees. An area the size of your living room could contain several different species of ants—totaling thousands upon thousands of ants.

Although some of Earth's larger animals inhabit the rainforests, most of them are somewhat smaller than their relatives of the plains. For example, the Aberdare Range of Kenya is heavily forested, although it is surrounded by plains. In these mountains, African buffalo of the plains and the forest mix. Both are of the same species, but the forest buffalo are much smaller than those that inhabit the plains. Forest elephants also are often a few feet shorter at the shoulder and have more

Insects are the most abundant animal life in the rainforest. These army ants swarm over dead branches as they travel through the forest.

compact bodies than plains elephants do. Compact size makes sense in the forest, where animals have to navigate around the trunks of trees and tree dwellers must make their way through a green tangle. In contrast, the grasslands can support great herds of large creatures, such as the 60 million bison that once roamed the American West and the millions of wildebeests in east Africa. Grasses are more nutritious than leaves and can feed immense concentrations of large mammals. Because the grasslands have fewer plant species, however, they do not have as many kinds of animals as the rainforests do.

Flying Frogs and Giant Grasses

While animals in the rainforests tend to be small, some plants other than trees grow huge when compared with their related species. The largest of all grasses grows in the rain-forests. It is bamboo, which in some places can reach heights of up to 120 feet (37 meters). In South America, there are water lilies that are more than 6 feet (2 meters) across. And in southeast Asia, a brown-and-purple flower called rafflesia is, at 3 feet (1 meter) in diameter, the world's largest.

ELFIN FOREST

The slopes of mountains above lowland tropical rainforests are often covered with dense woodland. These montane forests contain many trees similar to those below, but at higher altitudes, they become smaller and smaller. On mountain summits, the trees are sometimes dwarfed, and they form what is known as elfin woodland.

One elfin woodland grows in the Luquillo Mountains of Puerto Rico, atop an almost 3,500-foot-high (1,068-meter-high) peak known as El Yunque. Wrapped in mist, bent by continuous winds, and clothed in mosses, the trees are gnarled and stunted. Species that reach heights of more than 50 feet (15 meters) on the lower slopes are less than 20 feet (6 meters) high here. Many of the trees have roots aboveground that resemble great claws and that draw moisture directly from the misty air.

Walking through elfin woodland is a strange experience. Fingers of mist snake around the twisted tree trunks. Leaves glisten with moisture. The ground is soggy and covered with green moss.

Scientists believe that elfin woodland is caused by a combination of factors. As it does below, rain falls daily on the forest. Yet even when it is not raining, mist, fog, and clouds screen out sunlight, obstructing tree growth. Strong winds, and temperatures that are much lower than in the rainforest below, also serve to stunt the trees.

Animals in the trees must be able to get about in the branches and travel from one branch or tree to another. A slim body helps, which is why many snakes manage to live above the rainforest floor. Among the most successful rainforest snakes are the emerald tree boa and the green tree python. They wait, coiled around a branch, until a bird comes near, then reach out and seize it with their long teeth. Both snakes kill their prey by squeezing and suffocating it, and both are as green as leaves, which camouflages them. The boa lives in

A woman in Sumatra, Indonesia, kneels by a rafflesia, the world's largest flower.

South America; the python, in Asia. Although they belong to different families, each one has evolved in a similar way, to adapt to the conditions of the rainforest.

Creatures that live in the trees, or arboreal animals, usually have body parts that help them climb. Most monkeys of the American tropics, along with a type of tree-dwelling anteater, have tails that can curl around branches and grasp them. This kind of tail, called prehensile, works like a fifth hand. Sloths, which live in South American rainforests, have large, hooked claws that enable them to hang upside down from branches by all four feet, which is the way they spend almost all of their time. The toes of tree frogs, which thrive in the rainforests, are tipped with suckers that stick to tree trunks and branches.

Left: An emerald tree boa grips its prey and kills it by suffocation. Right: In the Amazon, a two-toed sloth hangs upside down with its sharp, hooked claws.

THE FLOODED FOREST

During the rainy season, the rivers of the Amazon Basin swell with water. The water level may increase by 40 feet (12 meters) and overflow into the surrounding rainforest. Because the land is low-lying, up to 10,000 square miles (25,900 square kilometers) of forest may be flooded in one season. Trees hundreds of miles from a river may stand in several feet of water.

When the floods occur, animals that live in the rivers follow the spreading water. Fresh-water dolphins, turtles, and caimans swim among tree trunks. So do many species of fish, including pacu and pirambeda. And although it may seem odd, the berries, fruits, and nuts that fall from the trees and fill the water during the flood season are an important part of the annual diet of many Amazon fish.

A section of rainforest in Manaus, Brazil, is filled by the Negro River. Nuts and berries that fall into the water feed the many fish that are swept into the flooded forest.

Many arboreal rainforest creatures are great jumpers, a plus for travel through the trees. The flying lizard of southeast Asia has flaps of skin along its sides that work like a glider's wings. It can jump distances of up to 30 feet (9 meters). Another glider is the red flying frog of southeast Asia. When spread out, the large webs of skin between its toes serve as parachutes. This frog lays its eggs in a nest of foamy mucus, which it secretes onto a tree branch hanging over a puddle. When the eggs hatch, the tadpoles fall from the branch into the puddle. They develop so quickly that they are able to breathe air before the puddle evaporates. There is even a rainforest kangaroo that lives in the trees and is an excellent jumper. The tree kangaroo of Australia and New Guinea can land safely on the ground from a height of 60 feet (18 meters).

17

2

At Home in the Treetops

In the Luquillo rainforest of Puerto Rico, the umbrella-shaped crowns of the yagruma hembra tree often flash their silvery undersides when swept by the wind. Taller tabonuco trees are distinguished by their dark green leaves and white bark. These two trees are among those of the upper levels of the rainforest, where animals truly live in the treetops.

Life in a Penthouse

The treetops of the emergent layer are always exposed to the weather. They bake in the sun by day and cool off at night. During and after a storm, they are dripping wet. When the hot sun returns, water evaporates quickly from their leaves. These trees are exposed to rain and battered by wind, and most of them have tough, leathery leaves that resist the forces

Opposite:
A monkey-eating eagle in the Philippines perches on an emergent-tree branch, waiting for a victim.

With iridescent colors that come from millions of scales on its wings, morpho butterflies are among the most stunning of their species.

of wind and weather and hold in moisture. The trees of the emergent layer have won the fight for light, in which all of the rainforest plants are involved. They have managed to grow up through the canopy, into the full light of the sun.

Emergent trees are thinly spaced, often acres apart. Their crowns, however, are very large, sometimes covering as much as an acre. Since the trees of the emergent layer are so high and far apart, only animals that can fly or are the best of climbers can live in their crowns.

An Aerial World

As they do elsewhere in the rainforest, insects abound in the emergent layer. There are plenty of mosquitoes, including some that feed on the blood of monkeys. Among the most striking residents of this layer are the morpho butterflies of South America, which have an 8-inch (20-centimeter) wingspan that flashes brilliant blue in the sunlight.

Where insects live, insect-eating birds will also be found. Among the most numerous is the nightjar (a relative of the whippoorwill and the swift), which scoops up insects with its wide bill. For animals with sharp eyes, such as the eagle, the tops of emergent trees make wonderful observation posts. Three kinds of eagles perch on emergent-tree crowns and scan the canopy below for monkeys to eat: the South American harpy eagle, the African crowned eagle, and the monkey-eating eagle of the Philippines. Although they are not closely related, all of them have crests or crowns of feathers atop their heads, and all are very large, which enables them to overpower the monkeys. Like eagles, vultures have superb eyesight. Vultures also cruise the air above the emergent-layer trees, searching for animals that have died in the canopy.

At dawn, the rainforest of southeast Asia often echoes with loud, whooping calls that come from the crowns of emergent trees. These cries are made by the siamang, a species of gibbon and one of the few mammals that regularly use this layer.

Siamangs are
territorial and
cry out from
emergent trees,
alerting other
siamangs to
their claim of
an area. Here,
a parent and
baby swing
from a tree in
an Indonesian
rainforest.

BIG EATERS

High in the canopy of African forests lives the colobus monkey. It feeds mostly on leaves, which are poor in energy-supplying nutrients and not easy to digest. This diet has a great influence on colobus behavior. The lifestyle of the colobus, which spends much of the day resting and sleeping, helps it conserve energy. In addition, the colobus is larger than most other tree-dwelling monkeys: Large size lowers the rate at which a plant eater uses up its energy.

Even though the colobus monkey does not expend much energy, it still needs to eat a huge amount of leaves in order to fuel its body. It eats about 6 pounds (3 kilograms) of leaves daily. This means that when a colobus monkey is not sleeping, it is usually roaming the forest in search of food.

Most monkeys—in fact, many other mammals as well—cannot digest the plant fiber and certain chemicals in leaves. However, the colobus's stomach can. Its stomach is similar to that of a deer, another leaf eater. During digestion, leaves must pass through two extra chambers in the stomach of the colobus. This gives bacteria in the stomach more time to break down the leaves, and it makes digestion a longer process.

A black and white colobus monkey surveys the forest from a treetop in Kenya.

Siamangs call out to tell other gibbons that the area around the tree they are in belongs to them; it is their territory. And in Africa, colobus monkeys sometimes leave the canopy to feed on leaves in emergent-layer treetops.

Life on the Roof

The canopy layer is the roof of the rainforest. The tops of canopy trees experience the same weather conditions that trees in the emergent layer do. Like emergent trees, many of those in the canopy have tough-skinned leaves. The closely packed crowns of these trees are like a green highway over which animals can travel from place to place. Canopy dwellers have plenty of space—vertical as well as horizontal—in which to find food, to hide, and to mate, nest, and bear young.

Eighty percent of the organic matter used as food by rainforest plants and animals comes from the canopy. More than 60 percent of the forest's animals and plants live there. In the canopy, plants grow on other plants. Lianas, some 800 feet (244 meters) long and as thick as a person's leg, thread their way through branches almost everywhere. These huge vines begin as tiny sprigs on the ground. If a young liana somehow gets enough light, it begins to twist around a tree trunk. It struggles upward, toward the canopy, where it will grow large leaves to gather sunlight and moisture. Some large lianas get so heavy that they topple the trees supporting them.

Many rainforest trees can have scores of other species— sometimes numbering in the thousands—growing on them. Most of these are epiphytes, a term that is taken from the Greek words meaning "upon plants." Epiphytes are also called air plants, because they do not grow on the ground. They perch on trees, shrubs, and other plants and even grow on human-made objects, such as telephone wires. Many epi- phytes, however, have ground-living relatives; among which are orchids, cacti, ferns, and bromeliads, a group that includes the pineapple.

Liana vines can climb hundreds of feet to the tops of rainforest trees. In a Costa Rican forest, these trees are heavy with more than twenty liana vines.

Ponds in the Trees

Epiphytes perch almost everywhere on trees: in the forks of branches, on trunks, and in hollows and cracks. Some have roots that take moisture from the air. Some bromeliads are shaped like bowls and hold water—more than 20 gallons (76 liters) in some cases. They are like ponds in the trees. Birds and monkeys stop by to drink from them, and their water holds various communities of living things. Dead organic matter that falls into the water is broken down into nutrients by bacteria. The nutrients are used by the bromeliad, as well as by algae and other tiny plants living in the water. The water in a bromeliad can be home to protozoans and many other small animals, including water fleas, crabs, mosquitoes, worms, beetles, and frogs.

Tadpoles develop lungs under water as they change from water-breathing to air-breathing animals. Here, an arrow-poison frog carries its tadpoles to a water-filled bromeliad.

In South America, arrow-poison frogs use bromeliads as a nursery for their tadpoles. (They are called arrow-poison frogs because native tribes use the frogs' secretions to make poison for their hunting arrows.) These frogs live mainly on the forest floor, but they can also climb. During mating, the female lays her eggs on the ground or in a crevice low in the trees. She stays with the eggs until they hatch. Her job, however, is not yet over. The tadpoles then wriggle onto her back and stick to her while she climbs up into the tree branches and searches for a bromeliad full of water. When she finds one, she lowers herself into the water and remains there until the tadpoles detach themselves from her. She then leaves, and the tadpoles begin their development into air-breathing frogs, just as other tadpoles do in ponds on the ground.

Jungle in the Air

The old idea of a jungle being a place of tangled vegetation that is alive with animals may not hold for the forest floor, but it certainly does for the canopy. Here centipedes, spiders, and scorpions seek their prey. Even certain earthworms live in pockets of soil in the trees. Two birds that are common in the canopy are among the most colorful in the world: hummingbirds, in the Americas, and sunbirds, in Africa, southern Asia, and Australia. Although unrelated, these two birds have something in common: Each has adapted to a similar environment in a similar way. Each bird has a long bill that can reach into flowers and extract the nectar for food. As they feed, the birds pick up pollen, which they transfer to other flowers, thus pollinating them.

Like the sunbirds and the hummingbirds, the hornbills of Asia and Africa and the toucans of the Americas also have bills adapted to the same type of feeding. These birds eat fruits and nuts, which they pick with long, decurved (downward-curving) bills that are wide at the base and narrow at the tip, like snippers.

A green violet-ear hummingbird feeds on an epiphytic orchid in Costa Rica.

Many of the mammals that inhabit the canopy are small, even tiny. Small size is an advantage for getting around among the branches. The mouse lemur of Madagascar can weigh less than 2 ounces (57 grams), while the pygmy marmoset, a South American monkey, weighs less than 5 ounces (142 grams). Marmosets and other tree-dwelling monkeys need good hand-eye coordination so that they can grab branches quickly and land on a target when they leap. Squirrel monkeys, also of South America, have such excellent hand-eye coordination that they can grab insects on the wing. Not surprisingly, scientists have found that the part of a monkey's brain that controls sight and grasping is very large, much bigger than the portion that governs smell.

STRANGLERS OF THE FOREST

Some of the most unusual plants of the rainforest begin life as epiphytes. They are the strangler figs, found in the Americas, Asia, and Africa. Stranglers sprout from seeds that land in the crevices and forks of trees after being excreted by animals that eat the fruit of larger stranglers. Once a strangler takes hold, the tree on which it lives is doomed.

After a strangler sprouts, it sends out threadlike aerial roots, which grow down toward the ground. The roots absorb water and nutrients from the air. As it continues to grow, the fig sends out more roots, which thicken and begin to wrap around the branches and trunk of the tree. Ever so slowly, as they grow toward the ground, the strangler roots begin to cover the tree. Eventually, the roots reach the forest floor and enter the soil. As the strangler increases in size, the tree that has supported it disappears within its woody embrace. The grasp of the strangler is so tight that it crushes the bark of the tree beneath it, cutting off the flow of water and nutrients, as well as light. The tree dies, and the strangler becomes a tree itself. Some stranglers are huge. The largest is the Indian banyan, which can stand 100 feet (30.5 meters) high and cover an acre of ground beneath its roots. On record are a banyan tree with a crown 2,000 feet (610 meters) in circumference, and a banyan that shades an entire village.

A. A strangler fig sprouts and sends an aerial root toward the ground.

B. More roots are sent out, which begin to entangle the tree; contact is made with the ground.

C. The roots thicken and wrap tightly around the branches and trunk of the tree.

D. The original tree dies and the strangler fig becomes a tree.

The pygmy marmoset, one of the smallest primates in the world, has a body only a few inches long. Marmosets prefer the highest branches of the trees.

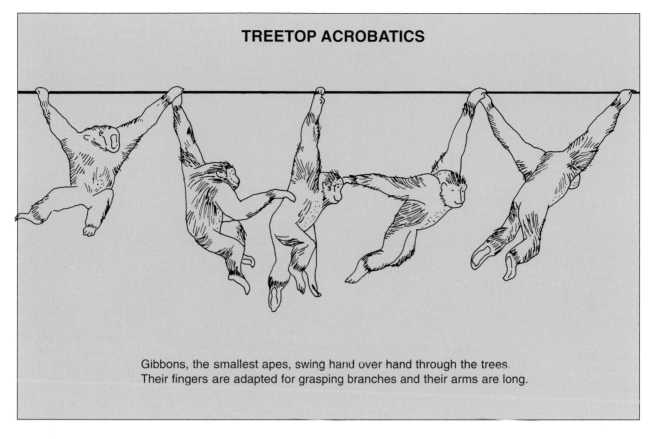

TREETOP ACROBATICS

Gibbons, the smallest apes, swing hand over hand through the trees. Their fingers are adapted for grasping branches and their arms are long.

A monkey's eyes, like a person's, see in three dimensions. Eyes placed in the front of the head, like headlights, are best for perceiving depth. They instantly focus on individual objects, important for judging the distance between branches.

Monkeys, apes, and people are the only animals that can move their fingers one at a time. The skin on top of a monkey's hand and under its fingers, like a human's, is full of nerve cells for sensitivity to touch. Their flexible, sensitive fingers help monkeys hold onto branches and pick up insects and other small creatures to eat.

Many monkeys almost never have to leave the canopy, because it provides them with all they need to live. Moreover, staying high in the trees keeps them out of reach of large jungle predators, which live on the ground and sometimes climb into the layers below the treetops.

31

3

Under the Big Top

Living in the middle and shrub layers of the rainforest is like living in the middle floors of an apartment building. There is not much of a view, and the ground is not too far away. Many animals that live in these levels frequently travel to the ground. Likewise, many animals that live mainly on the ground often climb to these levels.

Plant Life Under the Canopy

Living conditions under the canopy are very different from those on the rainforest's roof. The middle layer is shadowed, and the shrub layer is dark. Plants that grow in these layers must be able either to cope with shade or to grow quickly enough to reach the canopy. Many plants beneath the canopy are delicate: They are either soft-stemmed or are young, future canopy and emergent trees. They compete fiercely for light, but profit from the protection of the canopy

Opposite:
A gorilla feasts
on leaves under
the rainforest
canopy.

above. By the time rain penetrates the canopy to the layers below, the raindrops have lost the force that pounds the trees up above. Humidity and temperature seldom change much, which also benefits young and delicate plants. These plants face the greatest danger when a huge canopy or emergent tree falls, which may crush them beneath it.

Emergent and canopy trees are also part of the lower layers of the rainforest. Their trunks stand out like immense pillars. The shrub layer, in particular, is the area in which the buttresses of tall trees form. They are like the feet of giants.

Among the most common large plants that grow under the canopy are palms, thousands of different kinds of them. Here, too, are tree ferns, ancient plants that are ferns but grow as large as a medium-size tree. Anyone walking through a rainforest in the Americas is likely to come across a relative of the banana, called the heliconia. These plants have deep green leaves that can be more than 3 feet (1 meter) long and are easily recognized because of the brilliant red, orange, and yellow bracts at the base of their flowers. And, as elsewhere in the rainforest, epiphytes, including many species of ferns and orchids, are everywhere—even clinging to the trunks of canopy trees.

The heliconia plant is noted for its colorful bracts, or leaves from which flowers arise. Here, a snail rests on a heliconia that is not in bloom.

Flying Under the Roof

Although it is not as thick as the canopy, the middle layer is dense because it contains many small trees close together and young lianas climbing upward. The shrub layer

ANT FARMERS

Among the animals that travel up to the trees from the rainforest floor is a type of ant that actually farms its own food. Leafcutter ants eat a fungus that they grow on chewed-up leaves. These fungus gardens, huge mounds that can be 20 feet (6 meters) across and several feet tall, are contained within the ants' nest. A leafcutter nest can have millions of residents, making the leafcutters among the largest of all ant colonies. Each colony has its own queen, large and small workers, and soldiers that defend it with jaws that can bite through human skin.

Each day, long lines of large worker leafcutters depart from the nest to gather leaves. They follow trails over the ground, which they keep clean and mark with a chemical scent. The workers climb up shrubs and trees, from which they clip pieces of leaves. Each worker carries a piece back to the nest and puts it in the fungus garden, which is tended by a small worker. The small workers lick the leaves clean, weed out harmful organisms, and fertilize the garden with their droppings. Each year, a colony of 2 million leafcutter ants can use more than 2,000 pounds (908 kilograms) of leaves.

All of the ants in a colony come from eggs laid by one queen. Queens live a long time, and each can have 5 million young over twenty years. When a young queen leaves a colony to start one of her own, she carries with her a bit of fungus with which she will seed a new garden.

is less dense, but since it is almost sealed in from above, it lacks the wide-open spaces of the rainforest roof. Because they are hemmed in, the flying animals that dwell beneath the canopy have styles of flight different from those that live above. Few of them are able to soar. Instead, most of them fly from perch to perch rather than over long distances. Some, such as birds called manakins, a number of different wrens, and Pekin robins, flit about from branch to branch. Skipper butterflies fly with rapid wing beats over short distances, scooting from plant to plant. Other butterflies, such as the South American heliconius, fly slowly. Since they do not fly long distances, they do not need the speed of the morpho butterflies, which live above the canopy.

The lower layers are also home to birds that like to hide in thickets. One of these birds is the white-rumped shama of southern Asia. Like the mockingbird of North America, it is a great mimic of other birdsongs. Although it sings often, the shy mockingbird is more often heard than seen. The African touracos, which are the size of small chickens, use the middle layer in much the same way that ground birds use the forest floor. Touracos have strong claws and legs, which they often use instead of their wings to travel through the branches. They hop, skip, jump, and scramble with speed and ease. Young touracos know how to climb even before they are able to fly.

Going Up, Going Down

Just as people dwelling in an apartment building often go between floors, many creatures move between the different layers of the rainforest. The middle and shrub layers especially are visited by animals that spend most of their time on the forest floor, as well as by those that live in the treetops. In Africa, for example, needle-clawed bush babies—which, like apes, monkeys, and people, are primates—sometimes come down from the canopy. Gorillas and chimpanzees, which do most of their traveling about on the ground, often climb into the trees to feed and, in some areas, build sleeping nests. Small mammals called tree hyraxes, which feed on plant matter mainly in the canopy, pass through the lower layers on frequent trips to the forest floor. Some kinds of pangolin, a mammal covered with scales, regularly go up tree trunks in search of ants to eat. And pythons and leopards invade the lower levels in search of prey. The area between the underside of the canopy and the forest floor is the crossroads of the rainforest.

Some pangolins that live in the rainforest have tails that help them climb trees by grasping branches.

NIGHT WINGS

On Mount Tamana, in the Northern Range of Trinidad, are two deep, dark caves that can be reached by a climb through the rainforest. The opening of one cave is just a vertical crack in the mountainside, but you can walk down a steep slope into the cave. The other is a huge hole in the ground. To enter its depths, one must climb down a rope into the darkness.

These caves are the roosting place of some of the most abundant rainforest mammals—bats. With the aid of a flashlight, it is possible to view the bats of the Trinidad caves. Thousands of them cling to the cave ceiling and walls. When they are disturbed, the flapping of their wings sounds like a whirlwind. Their ghostly forms flit and dart about, swirling past the humans who have entered their underground refuge.

Walking through a bat cave is messy, slippery work. The floor is covered with a muck of decomposing bat droppings that sucks at the boots of anyone walking through it. The droppings are unpleasant to us, but as they break down, they turn into nutrients that are an important part of a cave food chain.

Many people fear bats. It is true that they can carry rabies, but they are not in themselves dangerous to people. In fact, the many kinds of bats that eat insects do people a great service. Although there are plenty of mosquitoes in this world, there would be many more if it were not for bats.

Other types of bats contribute to the growth of the rainforest. Like hummingbirds and sunbirds, these bats feed on the nectar of flowers. As they feed, pollen sticks to their bodies. Nectar-feeding bats then carry pollen from flower to flower, fertilizing them. Still other species of tropical bats feed on fruit. Some even catch fish in their sharp claws as they skim the surface of streams.

Of all bats, the subject of the scariest stories is the three kinds of vampire bat. Many cultures have legends about blood-sucking fiends called vampires. However, vampire bats live only in tropical America. Europeans had never heard of them until the Spanish explorers arrived in Mexico and South America. In fact, the name vampire was given to these bats by Hernando Cortés, the Spaniard who conquered the Mexican empire of the Aztecs.

Vampire bats feed on blood, but they do not suck it. First, the bat cuts out with its teeth a tiny slice in the skin of its sleeping host, which allows a trickle of blood to flow. Chemicals in the bat's saliva prevent the blood from clotting. The bat then quickly laps up the blood. Its tongue inverts to form a channel through which blood flows into its mouth. Scientists believe that the bite of a vampire has some kind of anesthetic effect because it seldom awakens the creatures on which it feeds.

Sambar deer and tigers are among the animals that roam the rainforest floor. They are large and, especially in the case of the tiger, impressive to see. However, they are just part of a much wider community of living things that inhabits the ground level of the forest.

Loners

Many people think that lions live in the African jungle. They do live in Africa, but not in the jungle. Lions are found on the plains, where there are vast concentrations of antelope and zebras, on which they prey.

Rainforests have far fewer large mammals than the plains do. Most of the animals that inhabit forests live in small groups or alone. The wild cattle of southern Asia called gaur live in small family groups. Tapir, found in the Americas and southern Asia, are usually solitary. So is the African bongo antelope. Most antelope inhabit the open plains, where there is little cover in which to hide. They use speed to escape danger.

tapir feeds on
ves and fruit
the forest
or.

4

Living on the Ground Floor

It is morning in the Khao Yai National Park of Thailand, where both the rainforest and the creatures that live in it have been preserved. On a sloping, grassy clearing, a herd of sambar deer grazes. Suddenly, one of them raises its head and gazes at an area along the forest's edge. Two white spots in the vegetation show that a tiger is there with its ears raised. On the back of each ear, tigers have a large dab of white. These spots, scientists believe, help the tigers locate one another in dense foliage. As the muscles of its powerful shoulders undulate, the tiger emerges from the forest and strides across the clearing, a few hundred yards from the deer. Now the entire herd is alert. Each deer has its head up and its eyes fixed on the tiger. However, the great cat is not hungry. It ignores the deer, reaches the end of the clearing, and disappears into the forest.

Forest antelope try to stay out of sight, and many have markings that allow them to blend in with the shadows. Other large, wary rainforest mammals include Africa's okapi (a relative of the giraffe), the giant forest hog, and the several species of deer found in rainforests of the Americas and Asia.

    Most of these creatures are the prey of the big cats of the rainforest: jaguars in the Americas, leopards in Africa and Asia, and tigers in Asia. Like their prey, the cats (with the exception of mothers with young) are loners. Because the animals they hunt are scattered and hard to find, they must patrol large areas to find enough food. Studies by scientists in India suggest that tigers may have hunting territories of between 25 and 500 square miles (65 and 1,295 square kilometers).

Jaguars are often loners and will fight each other over territorial rights.

41

The Hercules beetle is huge for its species and has a very unusual head.

Little Giants

Some small animals found on the forest floor are giants of their kind. Most North American centipedes are about an inch or so long. A centipede lives in South America that is more than 10 inches (25 centimeters) long; it feeds on mice and lizards. The Hercules beetle, of Central and South America, is 5 inches (13 centimeters) long. The Goliath frog of Africa measures 3 feet (1 meter) long with its legs out-stretched, and weighs more than 7 pounds (3 kilograms). It can actually swallow a rat!

Year-round Living

Unlike birds and mammals, reptiles and amphibians do not produce their own body heat. Instead, they take on the temperature of their surroundings. Reptiles and amphibians that inhabit regions and biomes in which temperatures vary drastically must carry on a host of activities to keep their bodies from overheating or becoming too cold. If these animals are cold, they must get into the sun. If they are too warm, they must find shade. In many places, such as most of North America, reptiles and amphibians hibernate during the winter.

Life is much easier for them in the rainforest because of the constant temperatures. This is one reason that a vast number of these creatures are found in the rainforests. Amphibians, moreover, need a great deal of moisture. Dripping-wet rainforests are amphibian heaven.

The moisture of the rainforest enables some frogs to lay their eggs out of water. Rattray's frog of South America places its eggs in a hole. After the eggs hatch, the tadpoles develop in the ground. Some species of frog in the Philippines lay their eggs on the ground. The young undergo their tadpole stage within the egg and hatch as miniatures of the adult frog.

Many snakes have markings that allow them to hide in the leaves of the forest floor. This helps them to escape from

WHICH CAME FIRST?

There is an old riddle: "Which came first, the chicken or the egg?" It may be impossible to answer, but we do know where chickens came from. The ancestor of the chicken is the red jungle fowl of the rainforests of southern Asia. There are more than seventy breeds and two hundred varieties of domestic chicken. All are descended from the red jungle fowl and can interbreed with it. When domestic chickens are allowed to run wild, after a few generations they begin to resemble the red jungle fowl.

Red jungle fowl inhabit forests and thickets of bamboo, up to an altitude of 6,000 feet (1,830 meters) and usually above 3,000 feet (915 meters). These areas are the montane rainforests. Like domestic chickens, the fowl nest and feed on the ground. Jungle fowl also cluck, cackle, and crow.

The fowl were probably domesticated about 5,000 years ago. People discovered that when they removed eggs from the hen fowl's nest, it would lay more. The Egyptians kept chickens at least 3,400 years ago. They built brick incubators that were heated by fires and were able to hatch thousands of eggs at a time. Domestic chickens were spread around the world. They probably reached Europe about 2,500 years ago.

Today, the red jungle fowl has become rare in many places. The main reason is that the forest in which it lives has been destroyed by human activities, such as the cutting of trees for firewood. Interbreeding with chickens also reduces the numbers of pure jungle fowl.

This Gabon viper, with its multicolored markings and flat body, is well hidden among the leaves of the forest floor.

enemies and to ambush prey. These include the huge reticulated python of southern Asia, which can grow to lengths of between 20 and 30 feet (6 and 9 meters), and the Gabon viper and puff adder of Africa. The viper and adder are venomous—they both deliver poison through their huge fangs. Their thick bodies are flattened, which enables them to lie very close to the ground, increasing concealment.

Hidden World

Many of the animals that inhabit the rainforest floor are hidden in its thick covering of leaf litter and soil. Although it is not obvious at a glance, frantic activity takes place there. The leaf litter and soil are the home of the forest's waste disposers. Fungi and bacteria continuously break down dead organic matter of all sorts into nutrients. Millipedes scavenge decaying plants. Dung beetles dispose of animal droppings by eating them. Land crabs consume dead animals and plants.

Even larger animals can hide in the forest floor. In Asia and Africa, porcupines sleep in burrows under the soil. And in the Americas, armadillos do the same. Lizards called skinks, many of which live in the rainforests, may spend most of their time burrowing.

A skink's body is perfectly suited for burrowing in the rainforest floor. Their pointed noses are used for digging and their smooth bodies slide easily through the soil.

Some animals that live on and under the ground are closely related to others that are generally found in and around water. Among them are polychaete worms, most of which are found in mud and sand on the sea bottom, and include bloodworms and sandworms, used as bait by fishermen. Planarian worms are abundant on the rainforest floor. Elsewhere, they are usually aquatic. These creatures can live on land in the rainforest because of the constant high humidity and shade. Without the cover of the canopy, they would dry out and shrivel up. Scientists have found that one of the strangest rainforest animals, the peripatus, can lose a third of its body weight in a few hours if it is kept in a normally dry room. This creature, which has been described as looking like a worm with feet, is believed to be a link between arthropods, such as centipedes and insects, and true worms.

Ants are almost everywhere on the ground of the rainforest. The army ants of South America and the driver ants of Africa can be dangerous to large animals. Both travel in bands that can have more than a million members and that attack insects, rodents, snakes, and even livestock. Ants, in turn, are the food of many rainforest animals, including anteaters in the Americas and pangolins in Africa and Asia. Although unrelated, these two mammals are similar in a number of ways. Both have large, powerful claws for digging up ant nests and long, sticky tongues for catching the insects.

Insects also furnish food for many rainforest ground birds, such as the red jungle fowl and the pitta of Asia, the bush robin of Africa, and the overbird, which breeds in North America and winters in tropical forests to the south. Many songbirds that spend the spring and summer in temperate parts of the world migrate to rainforests for the winter.

Rainforests are dwindling, due to human activities. If this trend continues, not only will rainforest creatures disappear because their habitat is gone, but so will migrating species that brighten the northern spring and summer with their songs.

DAY AND NIGHT

Some rainforest animals are active during the day, while others are active at night. Both at dawn and at dusk, a new set of characters takes the stage. Because only one group is awake and feeding at each time, a greater number of animals are able to use the same habitat without competing for space.

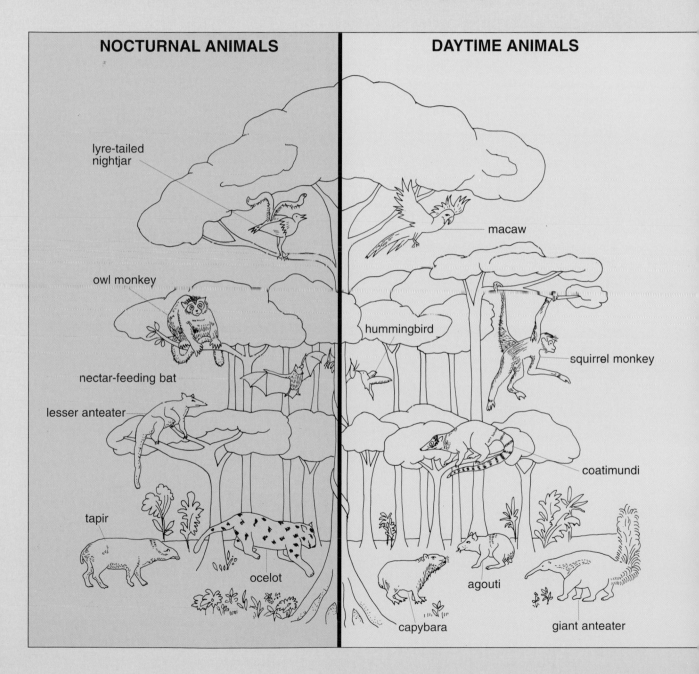

NOCTURNAL ANIMALS

lyre-tailed nightjar

owl monkey

nectar-feeding bat

lesser anteater

tapir

ocelot

DAYTIME ANIMALS

macaw

hummingbird

squirrel monkey

coatimundi

agouti

giant anteater

capybara

5

The Disappearing Rainforest

There have been many films and stories about people discovering live dinosaurs in jungles and other remote places. Of course, that has never really happened. In 1994, however, something nearly as sensational did: Within a remote rainforest in the Wollemi National Park of Australia, scientists found thirty-nine living pines belonging to a species of tree considered to be extinct since the days when dinosaurs ruled the earth. One newscaster called the find "a real-life Jurassic Park."

The fact that these tree versions of a dinosaur have survived is astonishing, and it is proof that scientists still have not found all the varied species of living things that inhabit the rainforests. Many other wondrous plants and animals may await discovery within the green interiors of the rainforest biome. Unlike the Wollemi pines, however, many species of rainforest organisms may not survive. Almost all over the world, rainforests are disappearing.

Opposite:
Logging operations damage areas of rainforest not only by felling trees but by destroying everything in their path. Here, a section of forest in Belize is being clearcut for timber.

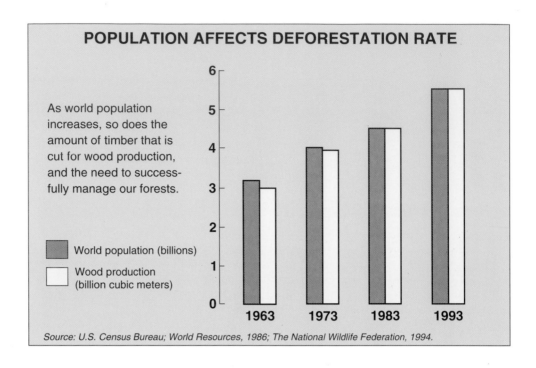

POPULATION AFFECTS DEFORESTATION RATE

As world population increases, so does the amount of timber that is cut for wood production, and the need to successfully manage our forests.

◼ World population (billions)

☐ Wood production (billion cubic meters)

Source: U.S. Census Bureau; World Resources, 1986; The National Wildlife Federation, 1994.

Shrinking Forests

Rainforests once covered about 7 million square miles (18 million square kilometers) of the earth's surface. Today only about half of that remains, and what is left is shrinking fast. Every year, about 50,000 square miles (129,500 square kilometers) of rainforest are destroyed. This is an area a little smaller than the state of North Carolina. According to some estimates, 19 million rainforest trees are cut down each day.

The greatest threat to the rainforests is from logging, for timber and paper. Hardly any of the lumber and paper products from rainforest trees are used by the people who live in the poor countries in which rainforests are generally found. Almost all of it is consumed by people in rich, developed countries, such as the United States, European nations, and Japan. More than half of the timber taken from rainforests, in fact, goes to Japan. In addition, most of the companies involved in logging are from developed nations. Many are from the United States, and almost half are from Japan.

Ironically, these same wealthy nations have begun to speak out about conservation issues and suggest that the underdeveloped nations now preserve their rainforests. But it is important to keep in mind that this contradiction stems from the fact that any one nation's government is made up of a group of people who have differing opinions regarding such complex issues.

Many people in the developing countries, however, feel it is unfair for conservationists in rich nations to tell them how to manage their own natural resources. In fact, it is true that many of the developed countries have already destroyed their own forests.

Some of the last original forests in North America, which grow in the Pacific Northwest, are now being cut for timber. Globally, there is a constant struggle to achieve a balance between supplying timber demands for economic reasons and preserving forests for environmental ones.

The rainforests of the world are being felled at an alarming rate. Trees that are hundreds of years old are cut down every day.

Anyone who visits railroad yards in rainforest countries can see the evidence of how many trees are being cut down. In Douala, Cameroon, for example, the yards are filled with seemingly endless chains of flat cars, each laden with massive logs that once were huge rainforest trees. Trains that have been unloaded head back to the forest for more logs. New, fully loaded trains arrive.

Part of the reason logging is so destructive is the way in which it is done. Logging roads are cut deep into the forest by bulldozers, which level everything in their path. Huge logging machines jockey fallen trees about and cart them to the railroad, destroying even more forest in the process. Although rainforests contain many tree species, the individuals of those species are scattered. Thus, loggers must cover a broad area to get enough of the species that are commercially desirable. They cut down not only the trees that they want but others as well, to get them out of the way. Once an area has been leveled, they move on, leaving behind a wasteland. Without the trees, the thin soil washes away with the rain and blows off in the wind. Soon, not enough soil remains for new forest to grow.

Logging opens up the forest to many other uses. Logging roads are often "enlarged" into highways, which make the rainforest accessible to large numbers of people. In the Amazon rainforest, for example, wealthy ranchers have turned great tracts of forest into pastureland for beef cattle. To do this, they have cut down and burned trees. The beef is sold to companies in developed countries, where much of it is used in the making of fast-food hamburgers. Poor farmers have also poured into the Amazon forest and cleared land for crops. The soil, however, is not suited to either ranching or farming. Grass grows poorly, so ranchers must clear more and more land to get enough feed for their cattle. The soil becomes infertile so quickly that farmers must move on and clear new areas every few years. As the human population of rainforest countries continues to explode, more and more people move into the forest in a desperate attempt to grow food. Therefore, the pace of forest destruction continues to increase.

Other threats to the rainforest include mining for minerals, oil exploration and production, and flooding, which occurs when dams are built to produce electrical power. Mining and oil production not only disrupts the land but creates pollution, a danger for both plants and animals.

Cattle graze in ever-increasing areas of cleared tropical forests.

Endangered Peoples

The Yanomami tribe of the Amazon rainforest is one group of indigenous people who have remained somewhat isolated and maintained their ancient ways of life.

Plants and animals are not the only living things threatened by the invaders of the rainforests. Because their interiors are so isolated, rainforests shelter some of the last so-called primitive peoples on Earth. These include groups of native peoples in South America and such tribes as the Penans in Sarawak, Malaysia. Primitive is not the right word with which to describe these people. They may not have televisions and supermarkets, but for generations they have lived in harmony with their forest world. As outsiders have entered the forest, however, the lives of these peoples have changed. Diseases new to them have struck. The plants and animals that have

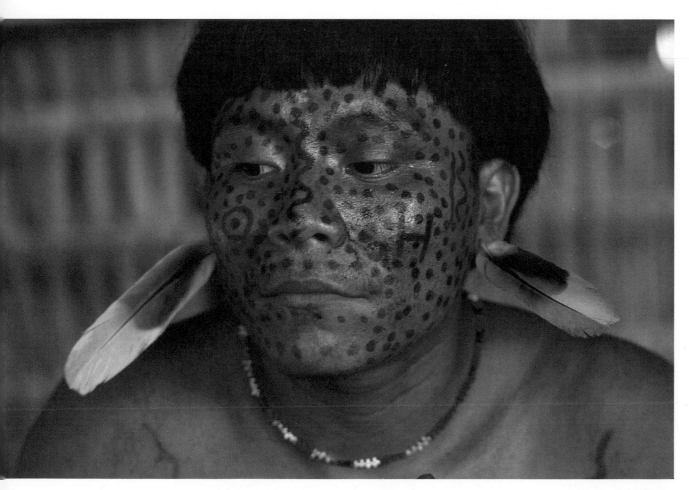

given them food and shelter have dwindled. Often, newcomers have driven native peoples out by force, and have even resorted to killing them. The way of life of these rainforest peoples, and even their very survival, is in danger.

Sometimes the persecution of a native tribe is aided by a government. The Penans are nomads who wander the Sarawak forest. They have no modern legal claims to the land. Most of the land they have used to survive on has been taken over by logging companies. In 1993, one hundred Penans stood in front of the logging trucks to block further entry into the forest. Malaysian government soldiers teargassed the Penans, then tore down their huts and destroyed their rice fields with bulldozers.

Saving the Rainforest

Stopping the destruction of the rainforest does not mean that it cannot be used for human benefit. There are many ways people can earn a living from the rainforest, without cutting it all down. In fact, over the long run, people will profit more from uses that are in harmony with the forest than from those that destroy it.

Tapping rubber trees, for instance, is not harmful to the forest environment. Neither is gathering nuts and fruits, which can be eaten or sold by the people who pick them. Farming fish and turtles that are found in rainforest streams is another productive approach. They provide far more protein per unit of space than cattle do, and farming them is environmentally safe. Although rainforest animals will vanish if their home disappears, not all have become endangered. It is possible that some species can be used to provide meat as long as enough individuals remain to keep their overall numbers from declining.

Some conservationists have suggested that areas of rainforest that have been cut down be planted with fast-growing commercial trees. This way, timber can be obtained without having to cut more forest. Another way to save trees is to

Tapping rubber trees is one way to maximize the benefits of the rainforest without destroying it.

make paper from plants that can be grown agriculturally. Vision Paper is a company in Albuquerque, New Mexico, that produces paper from a plant called kenaf, which is easily produced on farms in areas such as the southern United States. Kenaf, related to cotton, originally comes from the central African rainforests. It has been raised in Africa and Asia for thousands of years.

Rainforests can also be used by developing countries to bring in income from tourists. Costa Rica, which has protected much of its rainforests, is a favorite destination for nature-loving travelers. In that country, the Kuna tribe runs a rainforest preserve. Money spent by tourists there supports both the preserve and the tribe.

Conservationists in rainforest countries and developed nations are working to save the rainforest and its plants and animals. Many groups in the United States, such as the Rainforest Action Network and the RARE Center for Tropical Agriculture and Teaching Conservation, support programs aimed at protecting the rainforests. RARE scientists are working with Caribbean, Central American, and South American countries to create preserves centered around rare birds. The Rainforest Action Network works to educate the public about rainforests and has carried out boycott campaigns against companies that are destroying them. A major film studio in Hollywood stopped using rainforest wood on its motion picture sets after an Action Network protest there. The Wildlife Conservation Society has scientists in rainforests throughout the world. They are studying endangered animals and helping local people start programs to save them. The world's first jaguar preserve, in the country of Belize, was started by a scientist from the society.

Ecotourism has proven to be an effective way to preserve areas of the rainforest. Here, tourists on a river boat admire a giant samauma tree.

A NATURALLY PRODUCTIVE ENVIRONMENT

When you have ice cream made with real vanilla or eat toast sprinkled with real cinnamon, you are sampling products of the rainforest. Both the vanilla bean and the cinnamon plant originally came from the rainforests. Rainforests are the source of many things that have improved, and even saved, the lives of people around the world. The winged bean from southeast Asia, which is now being produced on farms, is an inexpensive and important source of protein for millions of people in poor countries. The bark of the cinchona trees of South America is the source of quinine, a medicine that has been used to combat the tropical disease malaria. During World War II, the lives of many American servicemen were saved by quinine. Also from the South American rainforest comes curare, a poison that native peoples there take from plants in order to kill animals for food. It has become an important medicine and is used as a muscle relaxant and painkiller. South American tribes also use a chemical called tetrodotoxin, found in the skin of some rainforest frogs, as a hunting poison. It is also used around the world as a painkiller. The rosy periwinkle, a rainforest flower, contains a chemical that has helped leukemia victims live longer.

Scientists explore rainforests for useful new chemicals from plants and animals. Once found, these compounds can often be reproduced in the laboratory and manufactured. However, they must first be discovered. The rainforest is a living laboratory that has only just begun to be tapped.

There are many uses for natural products of the rainforest. Rosy periwinkle flowers provide a chemical used for certain cancer patients.

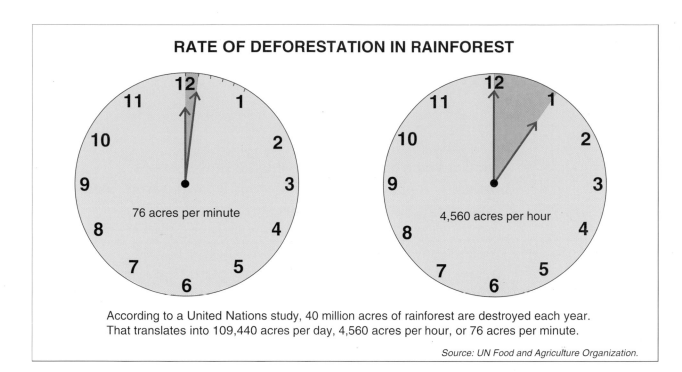

RATE OF DEFORESTATION IN RAINFOREST

76 acres per minute

4,560 acres per hour

According to a United Nations study, 40 million acres of rainforest are destroyed each year. That translates into 109,440 acres per day, 4,560 acres per hour, or 76 acres per minute.

Source: UN Food and Agriculture Organization.

Saving the Rainforest to Save the Planet

Of all the reasons to save the rainforest, perhaps the most important is the effect it has on the earth's atmosphere. When plants make food by using photosynthesis, they use up carbon dioxide and release oxygen. Rainforest plants produce much of the oxygen in the atmosphere. They also take in an enormous amount of carbon dioxide. In recent years, the amount of carbon dioxide in the atmosphere has grown. Scientists believe that two causes of this increase are industrial pollution and the burning of the rainforests. Some scientists believe that the buildup of carbon dioxide in the atmosphere plays a key part in a trend they have called global warming, a slow increase in the earth's air temperatures. If it continues, they warn, climates could change. The polar ice caps could melt, causing sea level to rise and flood coastal regions. Many areas of the world that support fertile farmland might turn into desert. Moreover, the air would become increasingly polluted. By saving rainforests, therefore, humans might also be saving the overall health of their planet.

Glossary

arboreal   Dwelling in trees.

bract   A leaf from the axil of which a flower arises.

buttress   A platelike growth of wood growing from the trunk of a rainforest tree that helps support it.

canopy   The second-highest layer of the rainforest, composed of the crowns of trees.

curare   A chemical from a rainforest plant that is used both as a hunting poison and an important medicine.

emergent layer   The highest layer of the rainforest, composed of the scattered crowns of the tallest trees.

epiphytes   A plant that grows on other plants.

herb layer   The floor of the rainforest.

Kuna   A native people living in Costa Rica.

monsoon   A season of very heavy wind and rains in southern Asia.

Penans   A native people living in Sarawak, Malaysia.

prehensile tail   A tail that can grasp.

quinine   A chemical from the cinchona tree, used to fight the disease malaria.

shrub layer   The rainforest layer immediately above the forest floor.

tetrodotoxin   A chemical from the skin of certain rainforest frogs; also used as a pain killer.

understory   The layer of the rainforest immediately beneath the canopy.

Yanomami   A native people living in the Amazon rainforest.

For Further Reading

Baker, Lucy. *Life in the Rainforests.* New York: Franklin Watts, 1990.

Gallant, Roy A. *Earth's Vanishing Forests.* New York: Macmillan, 1992.

Hamilton, Jean. *Tropical Rainforests.* San Luis Obispo, CA: Blake Publishing, 1993.

Hare, Tony. *Rainforest Destruction.* New York: Franklin Watts, 1990.

Leggett, Jeremy. *Dying Forests.* New York: Marshall Cavendish, 1991.

Morrison, Marion. *The Amazon Rain Forest and Its People.* New York: Thomson Learning, 1993.

Ricciuti, Edward R. *What on Earth is a Skink?* Woodbridge, CT: Blackbirch Press, 1994.

_____. *What on Earth is a Capybara?* Woodbridge, CT: Blackbirch Press, 1995.

_____. *What on Earth is a Pangolin?* Woodbridge, CT: Blackbirch Press, 1994.

Warburton, Lois. *Rainforests.* San Diego, CA: Lucent Books, 1991.

Williams, Lawrence. *Jungles.* New York: Marshall Cavendish, 1990.

Index

Acknowledgments and Photo Credits

Cover and page 57: ©Will and Deni McIntyre/Photo Researchers, Inc.; p. 7: ©Robert A. Lubeck/Earth Scenes; p. 11: ©Karl Weidmann/Photo Researchers, Inc.; p. 14: ©G. I. Bernard/Animals Animals; p. 15: ©Adrienne T. Gibson/Earth Scenes; pp. 16 (left), 40: ©Jany Sauvanet/Photo Researchers, Inc.; pp. 16 (right), 17, 20, 41: ©Luiz Claudio Marigo/Peter Arnold, Inc.; p. 18: ©Ziesler/Jacana/Photo Researchers, Inc.; p. 22: ©Tom McHugh/Photo Researchers, Inc.; p. 23: ©Mark Boultron/Photo Researchers, Inc.; p. 25: ©Ronald Orenstein/Earth Scenes; pp. 26, 28: ©Michael Fogden/Animals Animals; p. 30: ©Gunter Ziesler/Peter Arnold, Inc.; p. 32: ©Bildarchiv/OKAPIA/Photo Researchers, Inc.; p. 34: ©Sophy Pilkington/Earth Scenes; p. 36: ©Roland Seitre/Peter Arnold, Inc.; p. 38: ©Gerard Lacz/Peter Arnold, Inc.; p. 42: ©E. R. Degginger/Animals Animals; p. 44: ©Gregory G. Dimijian/Photo Researchers, Inc.; p. 45: ©Photo Researchers, Inc.; p. 48: ©Michael J. Balick/Peter Arnold, Inc.; p. 51: ©BIOS/M. Gunther/Animals Animals; p. 53: ©Dr. Nigel Smith/Animals Animals; p. 54: ©Victor Englebert/Photo Researchers, Inc.; p. 56: ©Paolo Koch/Photo Researchers, Inc.; p. 58: ©Richard Parker/Photo Researchers, Inc.
Artwork and graphics by Blackbirch Graphics, Inc.